T0065377

A Pocketbook of

God's
Promises
in a
Pandemic

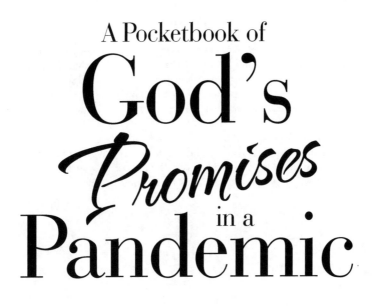

PRISCILLA CALCOTE

WESTBOW
P R E S S®
A DIVISION OF THOMAS NELSON
& ZONDERVAN

This book is a work of non-fiction. Unless otherwise noted, the author
and the publisher make no explicit guarantees as to the accuracy of
the information contained in this book and in some cases, names
of people and places have been altered to protect their privacy.

WestBow Press books may be ordered through
booksellers or by contacting:

WestBow Press
A Division of Thomas Nelson & Zondervan
1663 Liberty Drive
Bloomington, IN 47403
www.westbowpress.com
844-714-3454

ISBN: 978-1-6642-0871-1 (sc)
ISBN: 978-1-6642-0870-4 (e)

Library of Congress Control Number: 2020920029

Print information available on the last page.

WestBow Press rev. date: 11/19/2020

And he said to them, "When I sent you out with no money bag or knapsack or sandals, did you lack anything?" They said, "Nothing."

Luke 22:35 ESV

Dedication

This book
is dedicated to
those who may
need a reminder
of who
to
Depend
on during this
Pandemic

Foreword

First and foremost I give God all Praise, Honor and Glory. This is the day that the Lord has made and I will rejoice and be glad in it.

To my cousin Priscilla, I just want to say that you have been a blessing to me and an encourager. We may be states apart, but your text messages have brought us closer together. You have encouraged, uplifted and have even put a smile on my face even when I didn't feel like smiling.

God has sent you into my life at a time like this when I didn't feel like I had anyone to hear my cry after my two best friends/sisters went to be with the Lord.

I know that you will touch many lives through your books because you have the heart of Jesus. People may think encouragement comes from someone outside their family but God has brought two cousins together at a time like this, so Thank You.

To the readers of this book, just sit back, open your heart and let God speak to you as you read the Word that God has given this Amazing Woman of God.

To God Be The Glory
Barbara Burson

Acknowledgements

First I would like to acknowledge my one and only Savior Jesus Christ for His unconditional love and faithfulness in my life. In 2011, God spoke to me and He has not stopped speaking and that is why I am here today in the midst of this 2020 Pandemic sharing God's Promises in a powerful pocket size book.

Secondly, I would like to acknowledge my daughter Chloe' who is now a 21 year old senior in college. She has made me a Proud Mama Bear. Eight years ago when our lives changed, I asked in prayer, for God to take care of her but God did exceedingly and abundantly more than I could ever ask. He blossomed her into a beautiful, intelligent, confident, independent, loving and God fearing young lady. And more importantly he pulled her close to him and today she has her own personal relationship with him. Nobody but God.

Thirdly, I would like to acknowledge my Pastor, James T. Meeks and The First Lady Jamell Meeks for their many years of love and service to Salem Baptist Church of Chicago. During this Pandemic Pastor diligently dedicated his time to not only ministering the Word through television and via social media but bringing forth "Faith in Crisis" which provided much needed information to the homes of many at the onset of this pandemic 3-5 days a week in March and April of 2020. His servant's heart brought God's Peace to those who may have been wavering in their faith. Thank you Pastor Meeks. Also, Thank you Pastor and your Salem team for planning and bringing forth prior to the Pandemic the six week growth classes that were offered on Wednesday nights at the church and extended beyond via zoom during the Pandemic on Prayer taught by Minister C. Terrell Wheat. Again, Thank you all.

Fourthly, I would like to acknowledge and thank Minister C. Terrell Wheat. He has been a blessing to me. He is such an obedient servant of God and his teachings are priceless. Nobody but God. His teaching on prayer has truly increased my prayer life and my walk with Christ. During the month of August 2020 I joined him and many others to complete a goal in 31 days, my goal started off at one thing and ended with this book. Nobody but God's divine order! Thank you Minister Terrell for your obedience to God.

Fifth, I would like to acknowledge the greatest group of Salem teachers that faithfully ministered the Word of God weekly every Sunday during the pandemic after Sermon Sunday school class. Michele Pullen, Michelle Strader and Van Johnson. This group of amazing anointed servants of God teachings has reshaped and reset my way of walking with Christ. Thank you all.

Finally, to my earthly Angels my parents Walter and Peggy Lawson. Mom and Dad, I thank God for allowing me to be your daughter, proof of God's love for me. Thank you both for your unconditional love and support during my 54 years of life. Nobody but God.

Pandemic

A disease that is prevalent over a whole country or world.

The antidote for any storm including a Pandemic is to

PRAY

P resence **R** est **A** ccept **Y** ield

"For God's **Presence** which brings forth **Rest** and allows us to hear and **Accept** His Word which transforms our minds to not lean on our own understanding but **Yield** to His will."

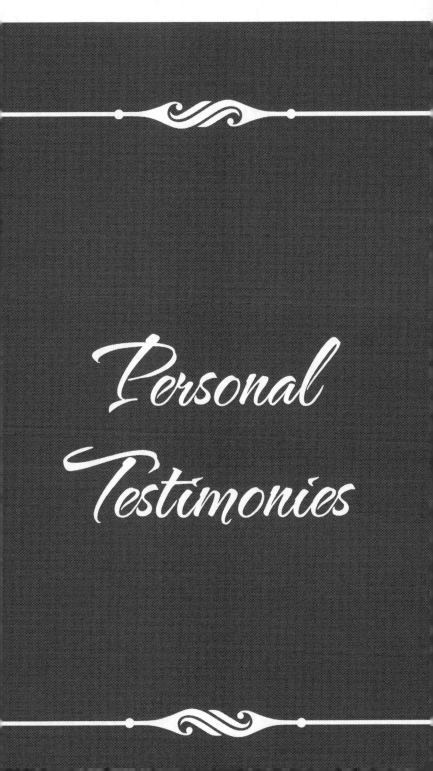

Personal Testimonies

The Presence of God is my Promise

As I recall my healing process, God has covered me. I can truly say I am blessed by God's Grace, Favor and Mercy.

My story began on March 24, 2020 I had initially broken my ankle which later developed an infection, which I then was told by the doctor that my ankle needed to be amputated. I was terrified. I had to compose myself immediately because fear had stepped into my spirit and I started to cry. But God spoke to my spirit and said, "Denise, fear will attempt to rob you of the good things (blessings) I have for you." Then I recalled a sermon from Joyce Meyer that said, learn how to challenge your fear head on and do it afraid.

God also said, "I have not given you the spirit of fear, but of power and of love and of a sound mind." 2 Timothy 1:7 KJV

I made a declaration with myself saying, " I will not fear: what can man do unto me?" Psalm 118:6 KJV

God also reminded me of Romans 14:23 KJV And he that doubteth is damned if he eat, because he eateth not of faith: for whatsoever is not of faith is sin.

I also believe the scripture John 6:29, "This is the work of God that you believe, adhere to, trust in, rely on, and have faith in God."

I kept reminding myself and saying, I Trust God, I Trust God, I Trust God. God has something special for me. God wants to bless me abundantly.

The next day I was smiling and ready for my surgery. Peace on my mind. I had no fear of my surgery or my future life. I answered fear with a step of faith. When fear knocked on my door I sent faith to answer it. I placed my Trust in God. I do not want to miss out on God's Promises for my life because of fear. I know God is a Healer and by His stripes I am healed. I will not fear, I am leaning on God's Promises. Glory be to God!

A Happy Amputee
Sister in Christ
Denise Roberts

God's Peace is my Promise

From Surviving to Thriving... this title was recommended by a coworker who was aware of the difficulty my family and I had experienced during this "unprecedented time."

I went through a turbulent time especially at the beginning of the pandemic. My husband had fallen and torn his quadriceps tendon, had surgery and wasn't able to walk without help. My mother lives with us and had much difficulty walking due to severe arthritis in her hip. I was a caretaker to both at home and working full-time being a kind of caretaker at work. I work with neurologically impaired patients. Family and friends would stop in to help or bring groceries while I was at work. When the shelter-in-place was ordered in Illinois, that help was now no longer available. I was fortunately able to take family leave and stayed home taking care of my mom and husband. Unfortunately, I also experienced anxiety I had not experienced in about 35 years. I was watching the news and looking at Facebook and hearing constant horror about the pandemic. My job, as I perceived it was "to keep the three of us alive". Very dramatic, but that's how I felt. Should I use this Lysol wipe now but I might need it later? I allowed myself only so much bathroom tissue because I had heard there was a shortage. I started conserving water, just in case. I especially went into panic mode when the governor asked for all healthcare workers to report. I was terrified of going back to work and being exposed to the virus and bringing it home to my mom and husband. My mother had always preached "one day at a time," but that was too much to handle. I was working on "fifteen minutes at a time." I asked God for Peace and Strength. I believe God sent me all kinds of help in different ways. I started doing yoga, downloaded a meditation app, and listened to positive podcasts, reading self help books, journaling, talking to positive thinking friends on the phone and praying, praying and praying.

After two and half months, I felt that I wanted and needed to return to work, which I did. My mom finally agreed to her hip replacement surgery and my husband started physical therapy.

I have been back to work for three months and I am glad. My 91 year old mother is walking now with no assistance and started driving. My husband is finishing up His physical therapy and is also beginning to drive and cook again.

We've been healthy, wearing our masks and social distancing and I Thank God every day. I have a long list for which to be thankful, so thankful for God's Peace.

J.A.

God's Promise of Patience taught me to wait on the Lord

Summer of 2019, I was searching for a summer internship that related to my journalism major and I had no luck finding anything. This upsetted me because I felt like I was wasting my summer and being unproductive. Little did I know God had something in store for me, God was teaching me patience. When I returned back to campus to begin my junior year of college I participated in a Greek step show and after introducing myself and my major, I was confronted by a man who offered me an internship position for the following semester at NBC news station. I was initially in shock because it happened so unexpectedly but I knew it was no one but God that sent him to the step show to meet me. In January of 2020, I began working for NBC and was able to learn new skills, meet new people, and gain new experiences. Also, I was compensated for all of my hard work, along with receiving not just 1 but 3 academic credit hours, which also was a blessing in disguise because I needed the extra credit hours from the internship to ensure that I would graduate on time in May 2021. No one but God.

Chloe' Calcote

Testimony of God's Faithfulness

In this Worldwide Pandemic of 2020 which began in late March with the sheltering in, shutting down businesses and the virus infecting many across our country. God has remained faithful and gracious to me. When the world relied on CNN I depended on God. He initially prepared me pre-pandemic by placing on my Pastor's heart to offer personal growth classes at our church on Wednesday evenings for 6 weeks. The class I chose was on Prayer. The minister that taught the class taught the purpose of prayer and how to have a private prayer life which has allowed me to come into the presence of God. This in turn changed how I prayed and what I prayed for and one of those things was **ME.**

I have always prayed for others and for myself but never specifically **God's desires for me, until now.**

At the onset of this pandemic I witnessed Christians having a " Peter Moment" which was puzzling to me.

"Come," he said, Then Peter got down out of the boat, walked on the water and came toward Jesus. But when he saw the wind, he was afraid and began to sink, and cried out, "Lord, save me!" Immediately Jesus reached out his hand and caught him. "You of little faith," he said, "why did you doubt?" And when they climbed into the boat, the wind died down.
Matthew 14:29-32 NIV

**Do you know anyone experiencing
"A Peter Moment" in this Pandemic?
Are you?**

The Word says:

But let him ask in faith, nothing wavering. For he that wavereth is like a wave of the sea driven with the wind and tossed.

James 1:6 KJV

List your Peter Moments during this Pandemic
(it's ok we all waver, But God)

1.

2.

3.

4.

5.

Now faith is the substance of things hoped for

(end of COVID -19)

The evidence of things not seen.
(God is in Control)

But without faith it is impossible to please him:
For he that COMETH to God MUST believe that
he is, and that he is a REWARDER of them that
diligently seek him.

(Consistent Prayer Time seeking his presence)
Hebrews 11:6 KJV

God is Able to do what he promised.
Romans 4:20-21

Do not drown in the sea/world of doubt, but have
faith that God shall deliver You! Take his hand.

Presence

So why was I puzzled about Christians experiencing The Peter Moment? Because at that time I felt we Christians should stand on our Faith and know God will deliver us from this storm. Then God spoke to me and said

"Priscilla everyone is not depending on me. I want you to share via text, testimony and in a book My 5 Promises."

Five Promises of God

1. **Presence**- Be strong and of a good courage, fear not, nor be afraid of them: for the Lord thy God, he it is that doth go with thee; he will not fail thee, nor forsake thee,
Deuteronomy 31:6 KJV

2. **Peace**- And the peace of God, which passes all understanding, shall keep your hearts and minds through Christ Jesus.
Philippians 4:7 KJV

3. **Protection**- No weapon that is formed against thee shall prosper; and every tongue that shall rise against thee in judgment thou shalt condemn. This is the heritage of the servants of the Lord, and their righteousness is of me, said the Lord.
Isaiah 54:17 KJV

4. **Provision**- But my God shall supply all your needs according to his riches in glory by Christ Jesus.
Philippians 4:19

5. **Patience**- I can do all things through Christ which strengthen me.
Philippians 4:13

Meditate on God's Promises for yourself at this very moment and list a time in this year 2020 that he has kept that promise. (Go back and if you have any Peter moments listed match it with one of these promises and see the faithfulness of God).

His Presence.........

His Peace...........

His Protection.......

His Provision..........

His Patience.............

During this Pandemic God spoke these five Promises to me which sustained me through the storm. June 30, 2020 all five promises were manifested. I can testify with a grateful heart that God's **Presence** shelters me daily. In His presence I have **Peace.** I no longer have fear of working outside of my home as a healthcare worker. In His **Protection** no virus or sickness came upon me in the midst of the storm. In His **Provision** an unexpected financial blessing was bestowed upon my daughter which assisted with the balance of her college tuition last semester. Finally, my change of heart, I was able to understand and have compassion for those who were doubting and wavering in their faith. God's demonstration of His Grace and Mercy towards me allowed me to have **Patience** with my fellow christians and to share God's Word.

God's desire for me to walk closer with him.

Do you know God's Desires for you?

Take a moment and Pray, come into His Presence and listen to him and list here what God is saying to you.

A Moment in Prayer

Rest

It is August 2020 six months into the Pandemic... the guidelines of the CDC are to continue wearing masks, social distancing and keeping six feet apart from others. I hoped as others in the world that our country would be flattening the curve on the rise of the virus and the death rate. Unfortunately other things have gotten worse along with the virus, unemployment is historically high, police brutality is soaring, daily protests over injustices and racial division escalating. All resulting from man depending on man and **NOT** God. The only answer for our weary minds and bodies are to seek refuge in God.

Four Reasons to seek God's refuge

1. Rest- Matthew 11:28-30
2. Reflect -1 Corinthians 11:24
3. Reset- Revelation 21:5
4. Reconnect 2 Chronicles 7:14

REST- Come unto me, all ye that labor and are heavy laden, and I will give you rest. Take my yoke upon you and learn of me; for I am meek and lowly in heart: and ye shall find rest unto your souls. my yoke is easy and my burden is light.

(God carries us when we can no longer walk.)

Even to your old age and gray hairs
I am he, I am he who will sustain you. I have made you and I will carry you; I will sustain you and I will rescue you.

Isaiah 46:4 NIV

Meditate and List a moment when you rested in the comfort of The Almighty God's arms.

REFLECT- And when he had given thanks, he brake it, and said, Take eat: this is my body, which is broken for you: this do in remembrance of me.

(Let's not forget what Jesus did for us on the cross)

Reflect over your life Pre- Pandemic the many blessings God fulfilled...

- If you were healed from cancer, what is COVID-19 to God?
- Established an eternal dependency on God.
- Sustained you after your divorce with a right mind, in the same job and house years afterwards.
- Removed the taste of alcohol and drugs from your body without rehab.
- Provided financially and never missed a meal or ever been evicted after you lost your job.
- Kept you in your right mind while God changed your spouse and restored your marriage.
- Gave you Peace of mind when your body image changed.
- Protected your daughter from being abducted.

- Protected your son from being fatally injured.
- Provided for your family when you had to care for your grandchildren.
- Gave you patience to trust him in the midst of all your storms.
- Gave you discernment along with peace to release people in your life who were only meant for a season.
- Regardless of your financial status or credit score God continues to provide not only your needs but also wants.
- **LIST YOUR OWN** _____

After reflecting, ask yourself is anything impossible for God?

If you answered No, then it's time to RESET

RESET- And he that sat upon the throne said, Behold, I make all things new. And he said unto me, Write: for these words are true and faithful.

(Accepting Jesus as our Savior we are Reborn)

Now that you were given time to Rest and Reflect in this Pandemic what is it that God is leading you to do? Is it your will or is it God's desires for you? There is a difference.

Make a list of your desires and afterwards state how it will honor Jesus.

Your desires   *How* it will honor God

1.

2.

3.

4.

5.

6.

7.

8.

9.

10.

If your desires are not bringing honor to God then you must **Reconnect**.

And the God of all grace, who **called you** to his eternal glory in Christ, after you have suffered a little while, will himself **restore you** and make you strong, firm and steadfast. To him be the power for ever and ever. Amen 1 Peter 5:11 NIV

RECONNECT- if my people, which are called by my name, shall humble themselves, and pray, and seek my face, and turn from their wicked ways; then I will hear from heaven, and will forgive their sin, and will heal their land.

(Restore relationship with Jesus)

Accept

You are asking How?

1. **Accept** That if thou shalt confess with thy mouth the Lord Jesus, and shalt believe in thine heart that God hath raised him from the dead, thou shalt be saved.
Romans 10:9 KJV

(Only Jesus Saves)

2. **Abide** in me, and I in you. As the branch cannot bear fruit of itself, except it abide in the vine; no more can ye, except ye abide in me. I am the vine, ye are the branches: He that abideth in me, and I in him, the same bringers forth much fruit: for without me ye can do nothing.
John 15:4-5 KJV

(We can do ALL things through Christ Jesus even in a Pandemic).

3. **Align** Trust in the Lord with all thine heart; and lean not unto thine own understanding. In all thy ways acknowledge him, and he shall direct thy paths.
Proverbs 3:5-6 KJV

(Trust Jesus He knows the plans for our lives even in a Pandemic)

4. **Act** What good is it, my brothers and sisters, if someone claims to have faith but has no deeds? Can such faith save them? Suppose a brother or a sister is without clothes and daily food. If one of you says to them, "Go in peace; keep warm and well fed, but does nothing about their physical needs, what good is it? In the same way, faith by itself, if it is not accompanied by action, is dead."
James 2:14-17

(Even in this Pandemic, walk by Faith and not by sight do the work and witness the goodness of God)

Yield

Surrender......

Then said Jesus unto his disciples, If any man will come after me, let him deny himself, and take up his cross, and follow me.

For whosoever will save his life shall lose it: and whosever will lose his life for my sake shall find it.

For what is a man profited, if he shall gain the whole world, and lose his own soul? or what shall a man give in exchange for his soul? For the Son of man shall come in the glory of his Father with his angels; and then he shall reward every man according to his works.

Verily I say unto you, There be some standing here, which shall not taste of death, till they see the Son of man coming in his kingdom.
Matthew 16:24-28 KJV

P   R   A   Y

Epilogue

*No unbelief made her waver concerning the
promise of God, but she grew strong in her
faith as she gave glory to God, fully convinced
that God was able to do what he promised.*
Romans 4:20-21 ESV

Printed in the United States
By Bookmasters